The Emperor Sigismund

F

THE

EMPEROR SIGISMUND

THE STANHOPE ESSAY, 1903

BY

ARCHIBALD MAIN

BALLIOL COLLEGE

OXFORD

B. H. BLACKWELL, 50 & 51, BROAD STREET,

LONDON

SIMPKIN, MARSHALL, HAMILTON, KENT & CO.

1903

THE EMPEROR SIGISMUND.

———

"His grand feat in life, the wonder of his generation, was this same Council of Constance, . . . the illustrious Kaiser,—red as a flamingo, 'with scarlet mantle and crown of gold,'—a treat to the eyes of simple mankind, . . . Kaiser of the Holy Roman Empire, and so much else: is not Sigismund now a great man?"[1]

Such is Carlyle's peremptory question. With the sure eye of an artist he has seized the outstanding incident in the Emperor's career and has painted it with greater skill than even an Ulrich von Reichenthal[2] could command. But he has done more: he has shown the historian of Sigismund where his task lies. It is not too much to say that, for him, all matters of moment centre in the drama of Constance, whether or not it be "one of the largest wind-eggs ever dropped with noise and travail in this world."[3] The Middle Ages were the battlefield of two great powers. The Holy Roman Em-

[1] Carlyle, *History of Frederick the Great,* I pp 190, 189, 186, whose account is based on Pauli *A P S G ,* II 74

[2] Von Reichenthal was a burgher of Constance who took some part in preparing for the accommodation of the Conciliar delegates He spent the last years of his life in recording his reminiscences of the Council, with special attention to its picturesque side His chronicle cannot be trusted in chronological matters L'Enfant and Von der Hardt have incorporated parts of it in their works.

[3] Carlyle, *ibid ,* I. p. 190.

pire and the Holy Roman Church vied with each other
for supremacy, and Christendom throbbed with the
conflict. The champions of the one could look back
with satisfaction upon a Canossa, but could little brook
the humiliating thought of an Anagni. The rivals had
fought many a fight, and now they were pitted against
each other for the last time on the shores of Lake
Constance. Never more did the whole of Latin Christendom meet to deliberate and act as a single common-
wealth with its temporal head in the full glory of his
international functions.[1]   Was Sigismund, then, the
knight errant of a dying cause? the wayward Paladin
of an Empire's waning splendour ?   Or was he the prophet of a new dispensation, heralding the dawn of an
epoch that would gladden the heart of a Dante?

It is no mere fanciful question. Constance was the
meeting-place of two worlds. There the ideals of the
Middle Ages trembled in the balance and the theories
of the modern era struggled for realisation. It is this
fact which makes the career of Sigismund, no less than
the beginning of the 15th century, so full of interest and
significance. Had this Council of Constance delivered
judgment against the old regime with no uncertain
voice, then it would have been easier to gauge the value
of the Emperor's high-flown pretensions.[2]   But the time
was not ripe, and the Holy Roman Empire had yet to
witness the neglect of an indolent Frederick III. and
the exploits of a chivalrous Albert Achilles. In truth,
the Imperial ideal possessed wonderful vitality. Its
roots struck deep in the hearts of men, and it is a
curious irony that no poet could outsing the praise
which Gunther Ligurinus, Barbarossa's enthusiastic
bard, lavished upon the results of Charlemagne's con-

[1] Bryce, *Holy Roman Empire*, p 334
[2] Cf R Lodge, *The Close of the Middle Ages*, p. 212.

quest.[1] Men could ill part with their cherished belief in a united Christendom with its temporal head, and even when their ideal seemed but a name of the past, it still exerted influence as a dream of the future. After each onslaught upon the claims of Hildebrand, the Roman Empire emerged more shrunken in territory and feeble in resources. But with Boniface VIII. fell the mediaeval Papacy, and men began anew to publish the gospel of temporal sovereignty.

The Holy Roman Church had aspired to a world-monarchy. In the words of Matthew of Vendôme[2]—

" Papa regit reges, dominos dominatur, acerbis
  Principibus stabili jure jubere jubet ",

and S. Thomas Aquinas quickened this conception of Papal power by his " De Regimine Principum " which pictured the relationship between spiritual and temporal sovereignty in a manner quite satisfactory to the former. But a reaction took place. Though the Popes were excellently fitted for the lofty position which they claimed not only by their sacred office and by the dread weapons at their command but by their " exemption from the narrowing influence of place, or blood, or personal interest,"[3] yet they had been tried and found wanting. Avignon cast an ugly blot upon their escutcheon, and Christendom turned with longing eye to the Empire Here was a power which might soothe a cruel disappointment and champion a growing hatred of priestly claims. Such a feeling had found expression in Dante's

[1] " Ex quo Romanum nostra virtute redemptum
      Hostibus expulsis, ad nos justissimus ordo
      Transtulit imperium . Romani gloria regni
      Nos penes est Quemcunque sibi Germania regem
      Praefuit, huic dives summisso vertice Roma
      Suscipit, et verso Tiberim regit ordine Rhenus "
Cf Bryce, *H R E* , p 218

[2] *Cambridge Modern History*, I 654.

[3] Bryce, *H R E* , p 268.

"De Monarchia"[1]—the dream of a pure spirit who
yearned after unity, peace, and order; the vision of no
"exiled Ghibeline but a patriot whose fervid imagina-
tion saw a nation rise regenerate at the touch of its
rightful lord."[2] Distracted by incessant strife, by
shameless tyranny, by hollow priestcraft, Dante passion-
ately bewailed the sorry plight of his country and
welcomed Henry VII., stranger and barbarian though
he was, as a God-given messenger of freedom and order.
Within a few years the champion of the Franciscans,
Michael of Cesena, joined issue with the Papacy by a
strenuous maintenance of the principles upon which his
order was founded;[3] and William of Occam, "the Invincible Doctor" of the University of Paris, lent his
erudite and ready pen to the growing outcry against
Papal claims.[4] From the political side the attack was
still stronger. Marsiglio of Padua, and John of Jandun
with boldness only equalled by acuteness, marshalled
argument upon argument against Avignon autocracy and
paved the way for a Constance and a Basel.[5] Had the
"Defensor Pacis" been the inspiration of an abler
leader than the vacillating Bavarian, the Reformation
might have had for its head a Louis IV. rather than
a Luther.

[1] Dante's was not the only voice   Aegidius Colonna and John
of Paris asserted similar claims   Their writings are in Goldast,
Monarchia S Romani Imperii, III   Cf Creighton, *History of the
Papacy*, I 35 n. (Edit 1897)

[2] Bryce, *H R E* , p 281

[3] Cf his appeal to a General Council, Goldast, *Monarchia*, III.
1360

[4] Cf Creighton, I 40   His works—*Opus nonaginta dierum, Trac-
tatus de dogmatibus Joannis XXII. papae, Super Potestate summi Pon-
tificis octo Questionum Decisiones*, and *Dialogus*, are important as
illustrating his position   Cf Raynaldus, 1323 (No. 38)

[5] Cf Creighton, I 42-3   Marsiglio's works are in Goldast (*e g
Defensor Pacis* in II 154)   Gieseler, *Ecclesiastical History*, IV. 26,
n. 15, gives an admirable summary of the *D.P.*

But as it was, the Papacy had a vitality even more wonderful than that of the Empire. After the Captivity her youth was renewed like the eagle's, and the literary attack was soon no more than an academic tirade.[1] The ancient glory of her rival had departed, and the comforting comparison of Gregory VII. was verified.[2] Yet the weakness of Empire was its strength. The pretensions which even the Hohenstaufen had failed to support, could never now be made good ; but with the growing sentiment of nationality so manifest in the early 15th century there still seemed a future for the head of Christendom. Could he be the arbiter of nations ? The Roman Empire was fast losing the very characteristics which now distinguished the Papacy. It was now "a power which acted from a distance and rested chiefly upon opinion," and "all visible manifestation of sovereignty fell to the share of the princes."[3] Feudal rights were hardly now enforcible, and direct contact with his subjects was no longer the Emperor's prerogative. He occupied an ideal position little affected by circumstances of birth or dynasty. He was still first of earthly potentates in dignity and rank, though he had no direct royal domain such as gave wealth to a King of England or of France,[4] and in resources would ill compare with many a vassal.[5] Christendom, however, looked to him— such was the tenacity of its faith in the Imperial ideal—

[1] *I e*, as far as revival of Empire is concerned, for Marsiglio's doctrines had much political influence.

[2] Ranke, *History of the Reformation in Germany*, (Eng. Trans., Austin), I 59.

[3] Ranke, *ibid* , p. 53.

[4] *Cambridge Modern History*, I 289

[5] *E g* , Charles the Bold, who desired Frederick III. to further his ambitious schemes of a Burgundian Kingdom , or the Visconti of Milan, who bought their title from Wenzel

as the type of spiritual unity, as the preserver of peace, and as the fountain of law and justice.[1]

All eyes were turned upon Sigismund when in Constance he had his great opportunity. Could he typify spiritual unity? Could he preserve peace? Could he uphold law and justice? If ever Christendom's ideal Emperor were needed, it was at Constance, and if ever the Imperial idea were to be revived it would be by one with a Sigismund's chance. There was that "monstrous parody of a Trinity in Heaven"—three Popes; there was fever of rebellion in Bohemia; there was an Italy of lawless and adventurous politics.

Christendom, however, had to suffer many a rude shock. The proud " King of the Romans " whom it went out to see proved little more than a reed shaken by the wind. But for Constance he would have been almost unknown to us, and his good fortune[2] only emphasised his conspicuous failure. The grim and petulant humour of Baldassare Cossa extorted by the snow-clad pass of Constance might well have been even more pointed—*sic capiuntur vulpes atque imperatores.* It would be unfair to deny to Sigismund some measure of success. His many " wise plans and good intentions " did not all miscarry. It was no mean achievement to heal the Schism, though he hardly counted the cost of his peace-making. But it is not unfair to say that, judged by the standard which he too glibly set for himself, Sigismund certainly failed. He is the self-sentenced Belshazzar of the Middle Ages.

[1] " Imperator Pacificus " was a title of the Emperor, *vide* Bryce, *H R E*, pp 270—1, notes.

[2] L'Enfant, *Histoire du Concile de Constance*, I 19, seq, gives an account of Pope John's negotiations for the Council, and tells how the imprudence of Cardinals Challant and Zarabella extorted some rather unchristian remarks " Sic capuntur vulpes " is more usually quoted than " Jaceo hic in nomine Diaboli."

Such an estimate of Sigismund's fitful career can be made good at every point, difficult as it is to thread one's way through the wondrous mazes of that career. In 1411, the eager and energetic Don Quixote of Emperors, quivering with Utopian ideas and fantastic plans, hastened to win his spurs in the lists of Church and Empire. The perplexities of the Conciliar movement, the perils of a Hussite Bohemia, and the intricacies of Imperial reform soon taxed his strength and tried his prowess.[1] Each, however, presented greater difficulties than Sigismund's mettle could overcome. Each proclaimed his signal failure, though there was not wanting the glittering tinsel of hollow success. Yet the years preceding 1411 are worthy of careful review by the critic of the Emperor's reign, since he must look to that period for the "genesis" and "revelation" of Sigismund's restless energy, lofty aims, and unscrupulous vacillation.

---

[1] It is difficult to deal with Sigismund's career   The older historians treated it chronologically without misgiving   Matthaeus' *Dissertation* (1723)   Cap I , *De Familia et Ortu Sigismundi*, Cap II , *De Provinciis hereditariis Sigismundi ejusque in iisdem Gestis*, Cap III , *De Gestis Sigismundi Imperatoris in Imperio Romano-Germanico*—despite his headings, is open to the charge   Engelbach's (1715), is a badly digested chronological summary   [It is noticeable that in them and in L'Enfant, &c , Sigismund is always "Emperor" after 1411, despite the fact that he was only crowned in 1433, cf L'Enfant, I 60]   Perhaps one may examine Sigismund's career in the way hinted above, *i e* (1) his training (1368—1411) , (2) Sigismund and Conciliar Movement, (3) Sigismund and Bohemia , (4) Sigismund and Imperial questions , though, of course, these (especially 2 and 3) cannot be quite separated.

I.
SIGISMUND'S APPRENTICESHIP.
1368—1411.

THE first forty-three years of Sigismund's life were by
no means auspicious. He plunged into the billows of
adventure and hardly surmounted one adverse wave
before he had to face another. Such a haphazard career
told its tale upon his future. When the tide of fortune
turned in his favour he found it well-nigh impossible to
cast off that shifty indecision, that incessant bustle, that
ignoble caprice and triviality which grew upon him as
second nature.[1]

His father, the Emperor Charles IV. and King of
Bohemia, has fared badly at the hands of historians,[2]
yet he was the most illustrious scion of the House of
Luxemburg, that House which acquired such sudden
but short-lived eminence. Probably he was the greatest
ruler of the fourteenth century.[3] "Step-father of the
Empire" and "Kaiser on false terms" notwithstanding,
his strong sense of political responsibility, and his tho-
rough business capacity, marked "the transition to
modern ideals and methods of government."[4]   Were it

[1] Creighton, I. 285-6

[2] Maximilian called him "the father of Bohemia, but the step-
father of the Empire" Bryce *(H R.E)* has said "he legalised
anarchy and called it a constitution" Carlyle: "Karl, a futile
Kaiser, would fain have done something to 'encourage trade' in
Brandenburg; though one sees not what he did, if anything " (I
173)   "Poor old creature; he had been a Kaiser on false terms."
(Ibid).

[3] Lodge, *Close of Middle Ages*, p 112.

[4] *Ibid ,* p. 113

only for the foundation of the University of Prag in
1348, a school of learning which could vie with that of
Paris upon which it was modelled, and which promised
to make Prag the unrivalled centre of Germany—were
it only for that beneficence Charles' renown was assured.
But he did more. He encouraged trade—the "Cheap
Purchase" against which Carlyle rails; he anticipated
the Council of Basel in his attempted union of the Latin
and Greek Churches;[1] and by his Golden Bull of 1356
he regulated the principles of election to the Imperial
throne and provided a check upon growing disunion in
Germany.[2] Charles IV. was convinced, as his son
Sigismund never was, that in pursuit of the "glittering
toy" of Empire the might of Germany was being
brought to nought, and he strove to keep abreast with
the rapid growth of territorialism. His intention was
to nurse the strength of the House of Luxemburg so
wisely that he would secure to his successors that pre-
dominance in the electoral college which would enable
them to govern Germany, and that overwhelming power
which would make good a hereditary claim upon the waning Roman Empire. If he failed to establish the Luxemburgs, he laid the foundations of Habsburg success,[3]
for his mantle fell on the shoulders of a Maximilian.

Charles had three sons, Wenzel, Sigismund, and
John of Gorlitz; and it was his weakness for them
which ruined his own wise schemes. Sigismund was
born on 28th June, 1368. His mother, Elizabeth, was
Charles' fourth and last wife, and gave this name to her
son (so the gossipy Balbinus tells us) as a grateful token
of her veneration for S. Sigismund the Martyr. The

[1] Cf. his foundation in Prag of a cloister of Slavonic monks from
Bosnia, Servia, &c.

[2] For Golden Bull cf. Hallam, *Middle Ages* (1869), pp. 298-9.

[3] For Habsburg possessions vide Lodge's summary on, pp
119-20.

Emperor betrothed him, while yet a boy, to Mary, the
infant daughter of Louis the Great, King of Hungary
and Poland, hoping, in due time, to enlarge the possessions of the Luxemburg family by the addition of these
states. Fortune smiled upon the ambitious Charles, for,
in the following year, 1373, Brandenburg fell to his lot.[1]
Three years later, in spite alike of solemn promise and
the provisions of the Golden Bull, he transferred this
latest province to Sigismund.[2] Even the third son, John
of Gorlitz, was not to be without his share of worldly
spoil. For him, Charles formed a duchy in Lausitz.[3]
But all such planning left the Emperor's most cherished
desire unrealised so long as hereditary succession was
denied to him.   Accordingly, he set himself to procure
the election of his eldest son, Wenzel, to the Imperial
throne, and after two years' unwearied diplomacy the
Golden Bull was set at nought[4] and his labours crowned
with hollow success. At Aachen, on 6th July, 1376, his
seventeen-year old son donned the robes of Empire.[5]
It was his last triumph, achieved but five months before
his death,[6] and it sealed the fate of the Luxemburgs.[7]

[1] There was a struggle for succession in Upper Bavaria, and
Stephen of Lower Bavaria, in spite of the 1349 treaty, obtained
recognition   Louis the Roman and Otto appealed to Charles IV.
for assistance and promised him the succession to Brandenburg if
they failed of heirs.   This agreement ultimately took effect in 1373,
when Otto ceded the province to Charles who promised never to
sever it from Bohemia

[2] Windecke, *Das Leben König Sigmunds*, § 3   The reff are to von
Hagen's edit (Leip , 1886) which is much more convenient than
that in Mencken, *Scriptores Rerum Germanicarum*, I 1074.   Windecke
was a native of Mainz (b. 1380) and was in Sigismund's service as
financial secretary   He accompanied him to Perpignan, Paris, and
London, but retired to his native town in 1424   His *Life* is the
work of a business man with shrewd and naive ideas   It contains
many inaccuracies, but these are remedied by von Hagen's notes

[3] Windecke, § 2   [4] *E.g* Charles IV. appealed to the Pope

[5] Windecke, § 2, n 1   [6] *Ibid* , § 2.

[7] For the break-up of the Luxemburg House cf Lodge, pp.
123, 119

Whilst the hapless, self-indulgent Wenzel, King of
Bohemia and lord of the Holy Roman Empire, was
struggling in the meshes of rampant Leagues[1] and Papal
Schism, Sigismund's opportunity came with the death
of Louis the Great in 1382, and "like an imponderous
rag of conspicuous colour" he was soon "riding and
tossing upon the loud whirlwind of things."[2] His ten
years' betrothal now promised him an exciting share in
kingly politics. Louis left a widow, Elizabeth, and two
daughters, Maria and Hedwig; and had persuaded his
subjects to recognise the claims of his children to the
succession. Maria was accepted by the Hungarians;
but the grasping Sigismund was eager to gain both
crowns with the hand of his future wife, and determined
to make a bid for Poland. The Poles, however, had
other ambitions, and would have neither connection
with Hungary nor a German ruler. They passed over
the prospective bride and elected her sister Hedwig, for
whom, in their zeal, they chose a husband after their
own heart, Jagello, Duke of Lithuania. This favoured
prince afterwards founded a powerful Slav state in
N.E. Germany, and, as he had no scruples against the
tenets of Christianity, cheated the Teutonic knights out
of a crusade. Disappointed in Poland, Sigismund's
whole energies were devoted to Hungary, but the "sub-
lime Hungarian legacy" proved small comfort to him.
" Delusive fortune," as Carlyle says, "threw her golden
apples at Sigismund, and he had to play strange pranks
in the wide high world."[3] Elizabeth, widow of Louis
the Great, was no Anne of Beaujeu. The sweets of
power made her loth to surrender authority to a raw
youth, and she did her best to alienate her daughter,

[1] Cf. Swabian League and League of the Lion.
[2] Carlyle, *History of Frederick the Great*, I. 178.
[3] *Ibid.*, I. 179.

Maria, from Sigismund, in the parental hope that, ultimately, she might have the reins of government in her
own hands.   Her decided preference, however, for
Nicolas Gara,[1] a minister of the late king, was a tactical
blunder which ruined her ambitions.   The Hungarian
barons, stung to the quick with jealousy, ignored Louis'
daughters, and turned for aid to Charles of Durazzo,
the nearest male heir.   Charles had won his way to the
throne of Naples in spite of Louis of Anjou, and might
well have rested content, but "the fabulous golden
fleece" of Hungary charmed more than a Luxemburg
prince.   The temptation to head a revolt overcame alike
the promises to a Louis the Great and the entreaties of
a Margaret.   Even the flight from Nocera was turned
to advantage, and hardly had the unhappy Urban VI.
set foot on the Genoese galleys when Charles, with a
few followers, hurried off to Hungary, and landed in
Dalmatia (1385).[2]   His first rôle was that of guide,
philosopher, and friend to the fickle Hungarians, and he
rapidly gathered around him a strong party; but he
soon assumed such kingly power that Elizabeth pre-
ferred discretion to valour.   In her sorry plight she
appealed for assistance to the youth whom she once
despised.   Aware of his danger and fearful lest Hungary
should prove another Poland, Sigismund acted with
vigour, and no longer delayed his marriage with Maria
(October, 1385).   The bridegroom had cast his die and
his face was now turned to Hungary—"that remote
fabulous golden fleece, which you have to go and con-
quer, and which is worth little when conquered."[3]
Young as he was he had not been without a romance,
but it was not a Burggraf's daughter who was to share

[1] Windecke, § 10, for history of this adventurer cf Windecke,
§§ 13, 20, 21, 60, 96

[2] Cf Creighton, I. 97.

[3] Carlyle, I. 179.

with him the glories and vexations of royal power. His first task was to raise money and troops for the defence of his wife's crown, and this he achieved by the doubtful expedient of "pawning" Brandenburg to his cousin, Jobst of Moravia.[1] While on this mission a crisis occurred in Hungarian politics. The silent tomb of the great Louis spoke, and in the moment of Charles' pomp[2] men remembered the good deeds of a king whose wife and daughter they had disloyally forsaken. Elizabeth took cruel advantage of the reaction, and successfully plotted the death of the newly crowned king in February, 1386. Her treachery cost her dearly, for the nobles of Croatia avenged the dead Charles by imprisoning her and Maria in the Castle of Novigrad, and when that fortress was besieged they put Elizabeth to death. Maria almost shared the same fate, but her husband, to whom the Hungarian nobles then turned, and who was crowned in 1387,[3] soon afterwards procured her release. His troubles, however, were far from ended, and had Eberhard Windecke been a Shakespeare he might have brightened his gossipy pages with the adage, "uneasy lies the head that wears a crown." The king quarrelled with his wife no less than his subjects; and Hungarian patriots sighed for happier times, when the Venetians seized Dalmatia and the Poles Red Russia, and when the Turks over-ran Servia, Wallachia, and Bosnia.[4] Yet Sigismund could not be accused of inactivity, and he made a bold bid for the recovery of these provinces. In 1392, the year in which his wife died, he conducted

[1] "He pawned Brandenburg to Cousin Jobst of Mahren, got '20,000 Bohemian gulden,'—I guess, a most slender sum, if Dryasdust would but interpret it   This was the beginning of Pawnings to Brandenburg "—Carlyle, I. 180

[2] He was actually crowned, 1386.

[3] Windecke, § 12

[4] Coxe, *House of Austria*, I 148

a campaign against the waywodes of Wallachia, but it was most disastrous in its consequences, for it indirectly involved him in war with the Turks. Four years later, though aided by John of Nevers and a band of French nobles,[1] Sigismund suffered a terrible defeat at Nicopolis. On his return there were disturbances in Hungary, and he was imprisoned for five months by the turbulent barons,[2] who, once again, sought a prince from the House of Durazzo. But Ladislas was too busily engaged defending his Neapolitan dominions against Louis of Anjou, to emulate his father's exploits; and on Sigismund's release there was a temporary truce.

About this time, too, Sigismund became involved in Bohemian affairs. Wenzel had not proved a worthy son of Charles IV. He might have been forgiven his neglect of the Empire, but he could not be pardoned his Bohemian misrule. Carlyle imagines that his talents for "opera-singing" and drinking Prag beer were notoriously in advance of his genius for monarchy.[3] His reckless passion, his ill-treatment of the clergy, his unworthy favouritism, were responsible for a series of Bohemian revolts beginning in 1387. Jobst of Moravia, "full of plans, plausibilities, and pretensions," a John the Baptist to the Sforzas of Italy, used every means to gain the crown by discrediting Wenzel, and even seized his person. John of Gorlitz came to his brother's aid, but his loyalty earned Wenzel's ingratitude, if not death by poison (1396). The scandals in Bohemia alienated the Rhenish Electors from Wenzel, who had given them fresh offence by pandering to the ambitions of Giovanni Galeazzo.[4] The luckless king had also fared badly in

[1] Cf Michelet, *History of France* (Eng Trans), I 311-12

[2] Windecke, § 13

[3] Carlyle, I. 176-7

[4] Creighton, I. 170   Three incidents. (a) Wenzel for 100,000 gulden sold Gian Galeazzo the title of "Duke of Milan"; (b) in

his spasmodic attempts to heal the Schism, and secured the goodwill neither of a cautious Boniface nor a stubborn Benedict.[1] At last steps were taken for his deposition. Four of the seven Electors met at Lahnstein in 1400 and elected one of their number, the Pfalzgraf Rupert, to be King of the Romans. The decree of deposition, read by Wenzel's opponent, John, Archbishop of Mainz, declared that he had not striven to end the schism, that he had not established peace or order in Germany, that he had abandoned Imperial rights in Italy. But there were deeper reasons. Wenzel's fate was really due to a Teutonic reaction against the French sympathies of the Luxemburg House, which had been so manifest since 1347;[2] to a reaction of the princes against the liberties of the cities which the Emperor had allowed;[3] and to the rise of that jealous oligarchical electorate which afterwards fought a Maximilian for constitutional control.[4]

Rupert was, in all points, a contrast to Wenzel. He was a just, upright, devout man, he had "a strong heart and a strong head"; but was "short of means" and, above all, had no military capacity. He invaded Bohemia, and was aided by Jobst, but withdrew after a slight reverse. Sigismund came to Wenzel's rescue when he saw hope of gaining another crown, and so managed affairs that he and not his incompetent brother was real master of Bohemia. Meanwhile Rupert attempted to gain prestige by striking a blow against the

1397 (two years later) the further title of "Duke of Lombardy" and the right of bearing the Imperial Eagle on his arms; (c) and the title over cities violently seized by him.

[1] Cf. Conference at Rheims, 1398—"a drunkard and an imbecile" met together. Cf. Creighton, I. 162, 154, 168-9. Michelet, I. 319-20.

[2] Yet cf. Lodge, p. 116.

[3] Cf. *Treaty of Eger* (1389).

[4] For effects of Golden Bull in creating this oligarchy cf. Lodge, p. 118.

power of the Milanese Visconti—"perched so high on money paid to Wenzel"—and by meriting the Imperial crown from a grateful Boniface IX., but he was easily defeated under the walls of Brescia (1401). Sigismund turned this failure to advantage and had it not been for Gian Galeazzo's sudden death in 1402, would have emulated Rupert's Italian schemes with much more chance of success.[1] Boniface, now thoroughly committed to the cause of the Pfalzgraf, made a counter-move by inciting Ladislas of Naples against Sigismund, and actually proclaimed him king of Hungary. But Sigismund acted with great vigour. By way of retaliation he forbade both in Bohemia and Hungary the payment of money to the Papal treasury, prohibited the publication of any Bulls, Papal letters, or ordinances, and strengthened this high-handed position by defeating Ladislas at Raab. He showed more than his usual wisdom, too, in his kind treatment of the Hungarian rebels, and, once again, maintained his kingly authority.

In 1408, Sigismund married his second wife, Barbara, the daughter of the Count of Cilly.[2] Some of the older historians,[3] delighting in details of domestic gossip, tell us that when Sigismund was imprisoned in Siclos[4] (1399) by the sons of Nicholas Gara he obtained his release by promising their mother he would marry one of the daughters of Hermann,[5] Count of Cilly, and so establish their position by kinship. Sigismund, however, was not happy in his choice of wives. Barbara fell

---

[1] Creighton, I. 174, relates the plans and counter-plans of Sigismund and the Pope.

[2] Windecke, § 20. Cf. Aschbach, *Geschichte Kaiser Sigmunds*, I. 122-5.

[3] Cf. Matthæus, who was steeped in the lore of Bonfinus, Gundling, &c.

[4] Aschbach, I. 124, 130, 132, 145.

[5] Not Frederick, as Windecke says. Cf. Aschbach, I. 262.

far short of the ideal woman, and would have justified
the cynicism of a Solomon. The ready pen of Aeneas
Sylvius, himself no mean judge of such matters, has
described her failings in pointed language.[1] No contemporary has written so gracefully or so frankly about
the romantic side of court life as this Lord Chesterfield
of the 15th century, a letter writer who could rival
Erasmus.

The year 1410 was, in many respects, the greatest
year of Sigismund's life, for in it one obstacle after
another was removed from his path. On May 18
Rupert " Klemm " died. Though a " highly respecta-
ble Kaiser " he had been quite unable to overcome the
difficulties which his position involved. That jealous
oligarchical electorate which had done so much to elect
him as a protest against Wenzel, had been too strong
for him—to use their words " they fell to plucking
the feathers from the eagle." With little congruity between profession and practice, they themselves had
neglected Empire as the luckless Wenzel had never
done. Burgundy rapidly swelled her dominions at Imperial expense. The process by which Brabant, Lim-
burg and Luxemburg were acquired by Philip the
Good, 1430 and 1462, was begun in 1406; all Nether-
lands, except Gueldres, Utrecht and Liége, were his;
and Franche Comté was to lead the way into Alsace,
Switzerland and Lorraine. The Electors, too, had left
the Teutonic Knights unaided against Poland; and denied to Rupert help against Milan. Indeed, Rupert
had not been really acknowledged between Rhenish and
South Western Germany.[2]

[1] Aeneas Sylvius, *Hist. Bohem.*, c. 59, and *Vita Fred III.*, p. 82.
For an embellishment of above stories see what the friend of Kas-
par Schlick says in *Parallelis*, l. 3, n. 44. It was he who said " I am
neither holier than David nor wiser than Solomon," and probably
he was correct as far as the first clause is concerned.

[2] Ranke, *History of Reformation in Germany*, I. 52.

At his death, the Papal "parody of the Trinity" was like to be matched by an equally bewildering parody in the Holy Roman Empire. Three scions of the Luxemburg family claimed the Imperial power; and Gregory XII., Benedict XIII., and John XXIII., had their counterparts in a Sigismund, a Wenzel, and a Jobst. The Schism was all the more distressful and dangerous as the claimants of Empire recognised different Popes, and this diversity of allegiance was shared by the Electors. Sigismund's was the patriotic and reform party, headed by Frederick Burggraf of Nurnberg who had saved his life at Nicopolis and was now his chief friend and adviser. The aged Archbishop of Trier and the youthful Louis, Elector of Palatine, adhered to this party. They looked to Sigismund to uphold Imperial traditions. His rule in Hungary, after an inauspicious beginning, had been very successful. He had compelled Bosnia and Servia to submit to his rule,[1] and had reduced the greater part of Dalmatia. Thus he could best aid Germany against the growing power of the Turks with whom, indeed, he had already crossed swords. He was heir to Wenzel of Bohemia and had the support of Bavaria, the great Wittelsbach House, through his alliance with the Palatinate. He was, again, bound to German ideas for support against the Magyars and Czechs. He was a man of culture,[2] of energy, of lofty schemes, and seemed the only prince with the power and will to do the needed work in Empire. His faults

[1] Windecke, § 19b , 20

[2] It seems curious that the Sigismund who was "super grammaticam" should yet be praised by Aeneas Sylvius for his learning, but it is so "   . illi liberalitas ac munificentia, quanta in nullo antea principum, religionis ac pietatis augendae studium incredibile, multarum etiam linguarum scientia, et in his linguae Latinae studium excelluit : quare doctos homines fovit .   accusavit saepe Germanos Principes, qui Latinas odissent litteras "—Quoted in Engelbach's *Dissertatio de Sigismundo et Albert II.* (1715)

of cruelty and sensuality, of shiftiness and vanity, were not yet so apparent and perhaps not much known beyond Hungary. Sigismund appeared the right man to lead Christendom and preserve its glorious traditions.

His party had a great advantage, too, in the prevailing contempt felt for Wenzel and Jobst, "the great liar"— as a contemporary[1] called him—"who seemed great, and there was nothing great about him but his beard." Yet Jobst had numbers on his side. His was the old selfish electoral party headed by "the hungry wolf," John, Archbishop of Mainz, and counted on the votes of the Archbishop of Köln, the Duke of Saxony, and the King of Bohemia, for Wenzel had never forgiven Sigismund his share in the deposition of 1400. On September 1, 1410, Sigismund by a diplomatic stroke for which his opponents were unprepared procured his election according to the strict letter of the Golden Bull.[2] But Jobst was not to be outdone. He saw no reason why Wenzel should object to promotion, and planned that his cousin should be recognised as Roman Emperor, whilst his own services should be rewarded by his election as King of the Romans. Accordingly, in October, Frankfort saw a new election and a third Luxemburg prince raised to Imperial authority. A doggerel rhyme concerning the three chief actors at this Frankfort election made much noise at the time and was hardly flattering either to the Archbishop of Trier or the Elector Palatine—

" Zu Frankfort hinterm Chor
Haben gewelt einen Konig ein Chind und ein Thor "[3]

[1] Jodocus Barbatus, 1411

[2] Sigismund repudiated his mortgage of Brandenburg to Jobst and claimed the vote which its possession involved. Jobst meanwhile had determined to stand by Wenzel and claim Empire on his cousin's death, and like Rudolph of Saxony did not go to Frankfort.

[3] Cf Eccard, *Corpus Historicum I*, 2144 Andrea Ratisbonensis, *Chronicum*

Such a situation boded ill for the sway of cherished ideals. Europe in the 15th century had outgrown the swaddling clothes of the Middle Ages.[1] But the glamour of Empire held Christendom in its grasp and its princes shut their eyes to the change of the old order. Sigismund was far from surrendering his claim without a struggle and was preparing to attack his cousin when Jobst suddenly died (Jan. 12, 1411). His task now was to reconcile his differences with the Electors, and this offered few difficulties to a man of his scruples. Wenzel was won to his side by recognition of his superior claim to the Imperial dignity, whilst the ecclesiastical conscience of Archbishop John was kept inviolate by adhesion to Pope John XXIII. Sigismund made matters secure by a third election at Frankfort in July. He recovered the fief of Brandenburg and showed his gratitude to Frederick of Nürnberg,[2] who had been his faithful henchman during the troublous Frankfort elections, by entrusting to him its administration.[3] Moravia was permanently annexed to the Bohemian crown.

Sigismund's Imperial apprenticeship was complete and the summit of his ambitions attained. These forty-three years of discipline are perhaps not the most interesting in his career, but they are the most momentous. Historians, no doubt, judge him by his share in the Council of Constance, "the Sanhedrim of the universe," as Carlyle has called it, by his inglorious

---

[1] For the humorous side of this pitiful schism in Empire *vide* Eccard, I., 2145.
"Adorant Christum tres Reges jam Romanorum,
Non sunt Tharsenses, nec Arabes, nec Sabinenses."—
Chronicum.

[2] Cf. Köhler's words quoted in Carlyle I., 185.

[3] Jobst had made the third mortgage in favour of the Markgraf of Meissen and now Sigismund has "pawned" Brandenburg for the last time, not without a substantial remuneration, 250,000 gulden, which made the total sum 400,000.

Bohemian policy, by his feeble attempts to anticipate a Maximilian of Imperial reformation; and probably these are fairly correct standards of judgment. But after 1411 Sigismund adopted no new rôle. His every action had its history. No more than any other mortal could he quite put off "the old man" and put on "the new." He learned from experience, doubtless, but the experience which taught, just as certainly moulded, him.[1] The French bishops at Constance were loud in their complaints against Sigismund's unscrupulous tactics, but would these complaints have surprised a Jobst? The leal-hearted John of Chlum could see the Emperor blush with shame at the mention of his futile safe-conduct, but was the brother of a Wenzel much nobler than a Ferdinand of Aragon?[2] Could one expect more from the shifty adventurer in statecraft than the feeble half-hearted reforms of 1427 and 1430? A modern writer[3] has aptly called Aeneas Sylvius a "pupil of circumstance," but the witty and learned Pius II. had many fellow-scholars, and Sigismund was one. The ever-changing and troublous politics of his early years found their counterpart in his restless energy and airy diplomacy of after life. He was ever active, ever needy, and ever dreaming. The Joseph of Emperors, he had already seen his relatives make obeisance to him and now saw in vision the sun, moon, and stars proclaim him "lord of all the world." Sigismund was the better for his dreams; they lifted him at times above the petty politics of his day. It was his misfortune that they were so fantastic.

[1] Cf. Creighton's remarks on the teaching of Sigismund's experience. They are not really contradictory of above.

[2] Eccard gives King of Aragon's letter, I., 2146. See p. 36 of Essay, n. 2.

[3] J. Neville Figgis in "Politics at the Council of Constance" in *Transactions of Royal Historical Society*, vol. xiii., new series, p. 105.

Thus an account of his early years has much more than a chronological value. No sooner was he elected King of the Romans than he startled Christendom by the audacity of his prolific plans. He made his debût by attacking the Venetians who had encroached upon Dalmatia, where Sigismund would brook no interference. After two years' tedious war a truce was arranged in 1413, and the ever restless King of the Romans seized the opportunity for striking a blow at the power of the Visconti. But he was not much more successful than the ill-fated Rupert, for Filippo Maria had strengthened his position after the assassination of his two brothers. Indeed, there was such "ludicrous incongruity between his pretensions and resources," that Sigismund was at once the most scheming and least successful of princes.

Fortune, however, was kinder to him than he deserved.[8] Pope John XXIII., warrior though he was, was sore beset on every side by Ladislas of Naples, the ambitious tyrant whom Boniface IX. had used so skilfully as a thorn in the side of the Luxemburg prince. But the Pope's extremity was Sigismund's opportunity. With characteristic zest, as newborn as it was suspicious, he championed the cause of Christendom and extorted from the helpless John the promise of a general council. The Holy Roman Empire was once more to lift its head and under Sigismund to assert the claims of an Otto the Great or a Henry III. The son of Charles IV. bade fair to justify the optimism of a disappointed Petrarch. Germany, and not France, was to be the "restorer of the Church and the arbiter of the Papacy."

[1] Appendix, Note A

II.

SIGISMUND AND THE CONCILIAR MOVEMENT.

How did Sigismund use the favour of fortune? Did he realise the expectations of Christendom and revive the ancient glories of Empire? At first he had serious difficulties to overcome. The Council had been called by a schismatic Pope and a dubious uncrowned Emperor.[1] Despite the efforts of Gerson and d'Ailly the Council at Pisa had been, on the whole, a failure. Apparently the times had not been ripe for the general withdrawal from the obedience of the rival Popes and there had been such perplexity of political motive that the position of the conciliar Pope was far from secure.[2] Again, John XXIII. had previously summoned a council to be held in Rome in 1412, but no one appeared to heed him.[3] Sigismund, too, might remember how Rupert III. had been treated at Pisa.[4] Yet on Christmas Day, 1415, the Council was a success. Amid unexampled pomp which must have satiated his craving for pageantry the Emperor, with a following of a thousand persons, made

[1] He was crowned at Aachen, November, 1414, though modern historians do not call him Emperor until after Eugenius IV. had crowned him. [But cf. Von der Hardt, IV. 23, for Pope's letter *calling him Emperor*, cf. p. 9, n. 2 of Essay]. Windecke, § 44. For descriptions of Aachen coronation see Monstrelet's *Chronicles* (Johnes' Edit.) IV. 74—79; L'Enfant, I. 60-2.

[2] Schwab, *Johannes Gerson*, p. 248, points out difficulties involved in 1409 Election.

[3] Raynaldus ann. 1411, § 7. Von der Hardt, II. 155. L'Enfant, *H. C. de Pise*, Pt. II. 93-8.

[4] " . . . a layman, and had nothing to do with matters of the Faith."

his first public appearance.[1] Frederick of Nürnberg as
Elector of Brandenburg carried the royal sceptre;[2] the
Elector of Saxony as Marshal of the Empire bore the
naked sword; and the Count of Cilly, the golden apple
of Empire. Sigismund attended early mass and, as
deacon, read the Gospel—"There went out a decree
from Caesar Augustus"—with befitting majesty and
pardonable pride.[3] After mass the Pope handed him
a sword with which he was commanded to defend the
Church. The Emperor made a solemn promise and as
L'Enfant grimly says "il l'executera bientot contre le
Pape lui-même, indirectement dans le personne de
Frederic, Archiduc d'Autriche, son Protecteur."[4] Sigismund had achieved a notable success. The Council
of Pisa had been a synod of ambitious prelates, but the
Council of Constance was the "Sanhedrim of nations."[5]

[1] For Sigismund's previous itinerary, Windecke, §§ 42, 43, 85, 44

[2] Creighton, I 312, calls him the Markgraf of Brandenburg, but as
yet he is merely Governor   The Margraviate was only given after his
part in securing Frederick of Austria, April 30, 1415

[3] Chas IV. had read the same Gospel at Metz in 1357   Mass at
Constance is described by Dietrich Vrie, in Von der Hardt, I 154.
cf L'Enfant's criticism I 75

[4] L'Enfant, I 76

[5] Cf. Gasquet *Précis des Institutions   de l'ancienne France*, II 20,
21, and Michelet I 469—76.   As regards numbers at Constance cf.
lists in Von der Hardt, V , pt. 2, pp. 11, 12, 28, 50   Gebhard Dacher
made his list at request of Elector of Saxony   He also kept a diary,
chiefly founded on Reichenthal's *Chronicle* and this is incorporated
in Von der Hardt, IV. L'Enfant, at end of his second volume, has
Dacher's list   John Hus, cf. *Historia et Monumenta* for his letters,
gives glimpses of Constance life, e g Ep V —"The living here is
very expensive, a bed costing half a florin per week " .   " we
lodge at Constance in the Great Square, near the Pope's residence "
    " I do not think the Emperor can be here before Christmas,
the council will be then near its close, unless it be broken up about
Easter "   Hus, at any rate, did not expect the Council to last for
more than three years   Alwin Schultz, *Deutsches Leben in XIV und
XV. Jahrhundert*, gives stray notes of town life, &c , which help one
to know what Constance in 1414 must have been like, e g pp 13—17,
20—23, 25, 31, 135, 145—148, 305—307, etc.

The historian can account for this remarkable dif-
ference. The latter Council represented a far deeper
movement than that which sought expression almost
six years before. It was an aristocratic revolt against
the Papacy from within and much more than the
ill-concerted disaffection of jealous Cardinals. The
Papacy itself had become hateful. Its ungodly Schism
and the rampant abuses which that Schism fostered,
loudly cried for reform;[1] and a Dietrich of Niem or
a Nicholas de Clémanges were but the spokesmen of
Christendom. Had William Durandus, nephew of the
" Resolute Doctor," been a prophet, he would have had
infinite satisfaction in the motto of the 15th century
conciliar movement. His words to Clement V. became
the watchword of reform. The Church was to be
purified "in head and members."[2] If one desires to
know how the Papacy was regarded by contemporaries
one has only to read the impassioned utterances of the
French or German reforming party.[3] Dietrich Vrie,
a German monk whose name appears among the wise
men of Constance, penned a Latin poem on the Church's
lost estate, and his historic reference to Simon Magus
sufficiently indicates its scathing character. The " De
Ruina Ecclesiae " probably written by Nicholas de
Clémanges, Secretary of Benedict XIII., rivals Hebrew
prophecy in the fierceness of denunciation, and its
sarcastic similes are the weapons of an Ezekiel. The
clergy are false shepherds; they care not one tittle for
their flocks; they would regard with greater equanimity
the loss of ten thousand souls than ten thousand
shillings. Bishops, monks, and friars are worldly,
dissolute, and shameless. This tract represented without

[1] For an account of Papal exactions, cf Creighton, II 120-5.
[2] *C M H* , I 620
[3] Appendix, Note B.

exaggeration the attitude of the French reforming party.
Dietrich of Niem spoke for the Germans. In his " De
Modis Uniendi ac Reformandi Ecclesiam in Concilio
Universali," he denounced the errors of the Church, but
he also advanced a scheme of reform. The power of the
Papacy was to be limited, one true Pope was to be
elected, the ancient privileges of the Church were to
be restored and all abuses removed. The utterances of
these men—and their testimony could be equalled by
many others—indicated a powerful, moral movement of
regeneration in Church and State when both seemed on
the verge of destruction. The rise of a Wyclif and
a Hus, the revolt of the Albigenses, the spread of the
Cathari—all pointed to a "wonderful stirring and
uprising in the mind of Europe,"[1] and the Council of
Constance was an outlet to the pent up feelings of
Christendom.

Sigismund's diplomacy, too, ensured the success of
the Council. The theologians of Paris had no small
opinion of themselves or their country. Gerson could
declare the French King the leader of civilisation and
superior to all earthly monarchs. The nation which
produced in Francis I. a candidate for the Imperial
throne was not likely to bow the knee to a king of
Hungary. But Sigismund, for once, had the wisdom
of the serpent. In his invitation to the French he did
not flaunt the "potentia imperatoria" but contented
himself with the "potentia regalis." He was the "ad-
vocatus ecclesiae," not her supreme arbiter. When
France was still chary of official representation at Constance, the Emperor in 1414 allied himself with the
Orleanists against the Burgundians.[2]

[1] Bryce, *H R E*, p 265

[2] Cf L'Enfant, *H. C de Pise*, Pt II 190—2 for (a) Sigismund's
Edict, (b) his letters to Gregory XII and Benedict XIII, (c) his

Then Sigismund's friendly relations with England stood him in good stead. John Forester was a connecting link between the chivalrous Henry V. and the Emperor.[1] Henry's father had sent an embassy to Sigismund in 1411, and English envoys had been prominent at the Aachen coronation.[2] If the University of Paris had a Jean Gerson, Oxford had a Richard Ullerston.[3] Accordingly Sigismund received much sympathy from England. He allied himself with Henry V. at Coblenz in 1414, and the lofty schemes of the English King led him to support the Council. In 1417, his zeal was so great that he could soundly rate his representatives, and encourage the Emperor to " finish the council and never mind me."[4]

Italy, France, Germany, and England, the four great nations, were thus represented, and the success of the Council assured.[5] Sigismund had taken the tide in his affairs at the flood, and everything pointed to fortune. On November 11, 1417, Oddo Colonna was elected Pope and the dark days of strife were ended. After forty years' wandering in the dreary wilderness of Schism the Holy Roman Church had reached her promised land. The Emperor, however, had not been without the fiery trials of a Moses. Before he was "lord of the world indeed " he had thrice to run the gauntlet. The first crisis in the history of the Council had reference to

embassy to King of Aragon; (*d*) his letter and embassy to Charles VI. of France ; and (*e*) John XIII.'s Bull for convocation of Council. Cf. Von der Hardt, VI. 8, for letter to Charles VI. For Gerson's and D'Ailly's views and difficulties cf. G. *Opera* II. 162, 810, 867, 885.

[1] *Vide* Rymer's *Foedera*, IX. 433.

[2] Monstrelet, IV. 75, 79. 91-2 for Constance delegates.

[3] Cf. L'Enfant, *H. C. de Constance*, II. 282.

[4] Letter, 18 July, 1417. Rymer, *Foedera*, IX. 466. Cf. L'Enfant, II. 98-9.

[5] Representatives came from Aragon, Oct. 15, 1416.

the deposition of Pope John XXIII.,[1] whose fate had
been sealed by Robert Hallam's rearrangement of the
method of voting.[2] The unhappy Pope refused to ap-
point proctors to carry out his abdication, and managed
to enlist the sympathy of the French against the insis-
tence of the more vigorous German party. Peter d'Ailly,
the Aeneas Sylvius of Constance, did all in his power to
embitter the French against the English and Germans,
and would have excited open revolt but for the timely
message of the French king. The seeds of mistrust and
jealousy were soon to bear much fruit,[3] and when
Henry V. set out against Harfleur (1415), the French
finally abandoned the reform party for that of the
Italians.

A curious illustration of these mutual jealousies is to
be found in the inspired protest of the representatives
from Aragon. Shortly after they arrived they were in-
cited by the French, who smarted under the German
"treachery," to cast doubt upon the position of the
English as a nation. The latter indignantly defended
themselves in a document bristling with quaint statistics.
Their monarch, they declared, ruled over eight king-
doms, his northern lands were as large as France itself,
his country counted one hundred and ten dioceses and
fifty-two thousand parishes (though the French could
boast of but six thousand), and his subjects had Joseph
of Arimathea for their father. Their suggestion that

---

[1] For accusations against him *vide* Dietrich of Niem *de Vita
Jo XXIII.*, II 3 (in Von der Hardt, II 391) "   multos arti-
culos valde famosos, et omnia peccata mortalia, necnon infinita
quodammodo abominabilia continentes contra eundem Balthas-
arem   . ." show their nature It was no wonder the Pope
" trembled "

[2] Appendix, Note C.

[3] L'Enfant, I. 117-120.

France and Spain should represent Western Christendom is as quaint as it is spiteful [1]

There was a second and graver crisis in the summer
of 1417, when even the English deserted the Germans.
The latter had consistently championed ecclesiastical
reform, insisting that the "causa reformationis" should
be prior to Papal election; and they had been consistently
supported by Robert Hallam and his henchmen. Sigismund and Henry V. had, up till now, been at one in their
policy and their ability to enforce it upon their representatives. Though the French had quarrelled with both
nations since 1415, they, too, had pledged themselves to
put Church reform in the forefront, and even as late
as November of the following year d'Ailly's voice was
raised on its behalf. But France had no Henry V. to
mould her policy, and her delegates had already shown
such disaffection as made them an easy prey to the
Cardinals. The petty jealousies of a Jean Petit squab-
ble had ruined the influence of Gerson, and the glamour
of the Curia had laid hold of d'Ailly. The galling sus-
picion that Sigismund and the hero of Agincourt were
using the Council to further their vaulting ambition,
was but another weapon in the hands of the astute
Italians.[2] Confident of a majority in nations the Cardinals protested against the Emperor's stubbornness in
delaying the Papal election, and their victory seemed
certain when his English allies deserted him. To Sigismund the red hats of martyrdom were as nothing to
this shameless defection. He did not consent, however,
to the new election until October, and before that time
events happened which make it extremely doubtful
whether, even then, he was defeated. His ally, Henry
V., was also a man of lofty schemes, and the prospect

[1] L'Enfant, II 37, 39, 44, 47   Cf. curious Latin poem fixed to
the door of Constance Cathedral
[2] Von der Hardt, II. 434.

of mediating between Church and Empire had many
charms for him, more especially since he was as little
interested in the reform of Papal abuses as he was
aided by the Treaty of Canterbury. Accordingly, he
despatched his uncle, Henry Beaufort, on a pilgrimage
to the Holy Land by way of Constance, and the sweet
counsel of a Bishop of Winchester atoned for the bitter
defection of a Bishop of Lichfield. Henry V. felt that
it would be a calamity were the Council to break up
without a Pope, and he knew that the Germans would
submit to such a solution rather than surrender their
position. Henry Beaufort explained his nephew's wishes
and won Sigismund to his side.[1]

The third crisis in the history of the Council concerned the method of voting in the Conclave. The
election of d'Ailly would have been a blow both to the
Emperor and Henry V., and they did all in their power
to frustrate the schemes of his supporters. The French
Cardinal, however, seemed a likely candidate. The
friend of John XXIII. as well as Benedict XIII., and
the leader of the Council, he could almost reckon on the
necessary two-thirds majority in the two Colleges of
twenty-three Cardinals and thirty deputies. But again
the pilgrim bound for Palestine came to the rescue.
He broke up the Curial party and set Rome against
France. Sigismund and Henry had won their Pope.
They had gained an adherent when they might have
crowned a foe. It was no wonder that the Emperor
threw dignity to the winds and humbly kissed the feet
of Martin V. In a cooler moment he might have
hankered after Imperial confirmation, but now he was
overjoyed and vented his feelings by telling Henry V.
how "the sun, the stars, the elements shout for joy."[2]

[1] Appendix, Note D

[2] Windecke had a good opinion of Oddo Colonna   Cf § 70
Cf L'Enfant, II. 159, 167.

Yet Sigismund failed at Constance. He had gained reunion under one Pope, but for this he had paid a great price. Oddo Colonna and not the Emperor had cause for thanksgiving. The Conciliar principle was maimed for ever and the Papacy entered on a new lease of life. The democratic revolt of a Basel Council would have no terrors for her champions.[1] The Holy Roman Church had escaped from the meshes of Council, Cardinal, and Emperor. Sigismund had signally failed to maintain his lofty position as arbiter, and two facts accounted for his failure. Constance was a nest of national jealousy, and the venom of national jealousy infected ecclesiastical dissension. It was a sign of the times that Church and State were so interlocked in unfriendly embrace that Conciliar solutions were all abortive. Sigismund had been powerless to check the patriotic hatreds of French and English. His well-meant expedition of peace had ended in a Treaty of Canterbury,[2] and he abandoned a friendship with France which his grandfather had sealed with his life-blood on the battlefield of Crécy. The Emperor had set his heart on Papal reformation, but he was too keenly alert to his own interests to forgive French designs upon Alsace, Lorraine and Flanders. John Forester can tell us what happened on Sigismund's return to Constance from the "Paradise" of England.[3]

[1] Cf. *Transactions of Royal Historical Society*, vol. XIII., *N.S.*, pp. 104-5. "The ' plenitudo potestatis ' rose like a phœnix from the ashes to which Gerson and d'Ailly would have reduced it. The Council of Basel, which had begun as a nuisance to the Pope, ended as a laughing-stock to Christendom." . . . "The Papacy was only strengthened for the struggle."

[2] For Sigismund's itinerary Windecke is important, cf. §§ 57, 82, 59. Monstrelet also gives picturesque details, IV. 213-218, 224-228, 247-8. Sigismund's motto, around a cross, when he went to S. Josse was, "O, how merciful God is." Lingard, *Hist. of Eng.* (1854) III., 249. Rymer, *Fœdera*, IX., 339-40. Michelet, I., 469-76.

[3] Rymer, IX., 434.

He shook hands with her envoys publicly, he constantly
wore the Order of the Garter, and he entertained the
English at a magnificent banquet. It was characteristic
of the Emperor that he busied himself in preparing for
war against his new foes. He induced the German
Diet to ratify his treaty (1417), he mustered men from
Hungary, he solemnly pledged himself to invade France
on S. John's Day, somewhat later he renewed his pledge
and vowed he would lose his kingdom and his life for it,
he even started shipbuilding on the shores of Lake Constance.[1] The effect of this change of policy is not
surprising; it sealed the fate of the Council. One can
forgive the shiftiness of a d'Ailly after the treachery of a
Sigismund.

These political interests, again, were at the bottom
of the ecclesiastical troubles. The orthodoxy of Jean
Petit's " Apologia " was a struggle of Orleanists against
Burgundians,[2] that of Falckenberg's a struggle of Teu-
tonic Knights against the Poles, just as the attack on
Hus was a German blow against the Slavs. The Papal
election itself saw an encounter of parties striving for
S. Peter's chair.

In truth, the Sigismund who had read the Gospel so
proudly at the Council's first mass, the Sigismund who
appointed guards, and granted safe-conducts, such as
they were, who determined the order of proceedings, the
Sigismund who so astutely turned the Swiss against a
recalcitrant Frederick or a fugitive Pope[3]—was not the
arbiter but the instrument of the Council. He was
" the secular arm " who could do the unpleasant work

[1] Yet in 1419 he had to get rid of Hartung von Chux, the incon-
venient confidant of Henry, by sending him to patch up friendship
between Teutonic Knights and Poles. Cf Wind , § 76

[2] Cf Monstrelet, IV , 93-4, 212-13   Michelet, I , 361-8

[3] Windecke, § 54

at Constance and who could be passed over when his work was done.[1]

The reasons which prevented Sigismund at Constance from making good his position as arbiter proved fatal to his claims to pose as reformer. The Council broke up without accomplishing its main object. The Sigismund of 1415, "with scarlet mantle and crown of gold," hurriedly left Constance, three years later, hopelessly in debt. He had soon found out that Martin V. was no tool for German hands and all he could show for reformation was the worthless Concordats,[2] the first-fruits of a Papal revival and the forerunners of the Pragmatic Sanctions of Bourges and Mainz. The failure of the Conciliar movement embittered the German nation and encouraged a Frederick III. to make an unholy alliance with the Papacy against reform both of Church and State. Sigismund's "wise plans and good intentions" made the German Reformation a revolution in faith, and the grounds of the Conciliar failure were the grounds of its success.[3]

[1] Cf. 1417, when the French turned him out of the council chamber.

[2] In Von der Hardt, I. 1055, *e.g.*, "Germanicae Nationis et Martini V. Papae Concordata," summarised in Gieseler, IV. 302, n. 19. Cf. Creighton, II. 110-2.

[3] Cf. *T.R.H.S.*, vol. XIII., *N.S.* p. 106, for an estimate of the Council of Constance. Probably the best way of viewing it is to make the Council one of many historic links—the Captivity, the Schism, the Conciliar Movement, the Hussites and the Reformation; and to regard them as national struggles against the *spectre* of Christendom. It is worthy of note that at Constance there are the same groups of nations as at the Reformation in Germany.

III.

SIGISMUND AND BOHEMIA.

SIGISMUND's failure at Constance haunted him for the rest of his life. His lofty schemes for the restoration of Empire's prestige were hopelessly ruined. The Pliable of Emperors he set out with brave heart and beating pulse for the celestial city of Imperial glory, but the "slough of Despond" had been too much for him, and he scrambled back to his native land. From the year 1418 he devoted himself to personal and dynastic interests, to defending Hungary against the Turks or enforcing his claim to Bohemian succession; and he preserved the traditions of his family by his neglect of Germany.[1] He even offered to resign the Imperial authority. It was an evil day for the "blushing" Sigismund when he handed over John Hus to the tender mercies of the Holy Roman Church.[2] The martyrdom at Constance "kindled Bohemia and kindled rhinoceros Zisca into never-imagined flame of vengeance; brought more disaster, disgrace, and defeat on defeat to Sigismund, and kept his hands full for the rest of his life."[3] The truth of Carlyle's words has often been confirmed. "From the flames of the stake of John Hus," says another writer, "a great fire was set alight which desolated Bohemia and Germany, and was only extinguished in the blood of countless victims."[4] Thus Sigismund's

[1] Ranke, I. 52.

[2] Cf. Haeberlinus, *Apologia divi Sigismundi* (1742), where learning of the schools is displayed in unravelling the Salvus-Conductus controversy. Cf. also L'Enfant, I. 403, and Von der Hardt, IV. 393.

[3] Carlyle, I. 191.

[4] Leger, *History of Austria* (Translation), p. 175. Cf. "Tot pingit calices Boemorum turba per urbes, ut credas Bacchi numina sola coli," p. 177.

troubles in Bohemia might well have been treated side by side with the Conciliar movement, but they were so momentous and involved such dynastic interests that they deserve more than passing notice. Their connection with Constance, however, must never be forgotten.

John Hus was but one name in the roll of a great revival which laid hold of Europe at the close of the Middle Ages. There had been many voices crying in the wilderness for spiritual awakening. Men were beginning to feel the yoke of Church authority and political scheming press heavily upon their souls. Gerard Groot, Florentius Radevynzon, Johann Tauler, John Wyclif, all testified in their own way to the needs of the individual life.[1] Bohemia was not without its witness, and Hus had his precursors in Conrad of Waldhäusen, Milicz of Kremsier, Mathias of Janow, and Thomas Stitny.[2] These men attacked the degradation of the Church, the vices of monks and friars, the wealth and worldliness of the clergy in high places;[3] and Hus was not a whit behind them when he preached in the Chapel of Bethlehem. From the year 1398, when he began to teach in the University of Prag, his confession of faith in philosophy and theology became modelled upon the opinions of the Oxford reformer, and though his fame does not rest on his intellectual abilities he seemed alive to the momentous consequences of Wyclif's teaching. "Oh Wyclif, Wyclif," he exclaimed, in a remarkable sermon, "you will trouble the heads of many."[4] His words were the words of a prophet.

[1] Cf. *C.M.H.*, I. 434-5, 627. Even at Constance Grabo referred to Groot. Cf. Creighton, II. 114. Ullmann, *Reformers before the Reformation*, gives most light on these men.

[2] Anne's marriage with Richard II. had established relations with England. Jerome of Prag had studied at Oxford.

[3] Cf. Andrew de Cesky Brod's scathing words quoted in Leger, p. 167.

[4] Quoted in Creighton, II. 3.

For twelve years, however, he was saved by Bohemian unrest. The anger of the slighted Wenzel against
Innocent VII. and Gregory XII , his temporising Pisan
policy, the strong sentiment of Czech patriotism,[1] the
unhappy Schism in Church and Empire, all stood Hus
in good stead and enabled him to brave the terrors of a
Colonna and an Annibaldi. But the politics of the day
could not always shelter him, and his Luther-like
denunciation of Pope John's sale of indulgences showed
that he could take a bold stand. On the invitation of
Sigismund and armed with an Imperial safe-conduct[2]
Hus went to Constance in 1414 to give a reason for the
faith that was in him. He had friends with him, but he
had also foes. The zeal of John of Chlum and Wenzel
of Duba was checked by the hatred of Stephen Palecz
and Michael de Causis.[3] His case was prejudged. England was tired of a Wyclif, the Papacy was bitter against
the Bohemian censor, Paris University was horrified at
heresy, and Germany was jealous of Czech nationality.
Hus, who came to convince Christendom, was condemned
to death. He had taught, so his accusers declared, the
necessity of receiving the Eucharist in both kinds, and
had attacked the doctrine of transubstantiation , he had
made the moral character of the priest a condition of the
validity of the sacrament ; he had taught erroneous doctrines respecting the nature of the Church. Sigismund
had, indeed, protested vehemently against the violation
of his Imperial safe-conduct,[4] but the straits of his posi-

---

[1] The exodus of Germans from the University of Prag shows this

[2] *Historia et Monumenta*, I , 2   " Honorabilem Magistrum
Johannem Hus—in nostram et sacri Imperii protectionem recepimus
et tutelam "

[3] It was Michael de Causis who " stuck up accusations " on the
church door   Cf Ep V , *H. et M* , I., p 7   But cf I., p 96, for
the efforts of his friends

[4] Von der Hardt, IV , 26

tion overcame all scruples.[1]   He felt that his reputation
was staked on the success of the Council, and that too
scrupulous a conscience would but yield victory to the
wily Pope John.   It was the acuteness of Peter d'Ailly
that completed his conversion to unseemly casuistry.[2]
Sigismund's desertion of John Hus had a moral which
he learned by bitter experience.   It showed that he
could be forced to do anything rather than ruin the
Council ; it proved that the Church could make "the
secular arm" do its own shameless work ; and it led to
the Hussite wars, the conspicuous failure of his reign.

Sigismund could never again lift up his head in
Bohemia.[3]   He was the perjured traitor of their martyr.
Hus had many enemies amongst his countrymen ; but
his earnestness, his piety, his patriotism, his naïve trust-
fulness, and, above all, his life-blood, endeared his
memory to the Czechs.[4]   Under the leadership of Nicolas of Husinec and John Ziska, a born general, the
Hussites soon became a power in the land.   "Communion in both kinds" was their doctrinal motto and
gave them their name, Utraquists.   In 1420 they formu-
lated the demands which became their avowed creed.
The "Four Articles of Prag" were (a) entire liberty of
preaching ; (b) communion in both kinds ; (c) exclusion
of priests from temporal power ; (d) secular discipline
of clergy.   Had Sigismund been a man of few and well-

[1] Von der Hardt, IV., 521.

[2] Creighton, II., 43.

[3] Even Wenzel was indignant at his brother's casuistry, but no
one can be quite sure of all the motives implied in a moral lesson—
especially that of a Wenzel.

[4] We find that Hus is not above a naïve punning on his name
(Hus-goose). *e.g.*, "The Combat is near, and the poor bird must
flap his wings against the wings of Behemoth" (as Bonnechose's
translation will have it).   There is a pathetic note in Hus' letter
from Constance to Martin his servant, to whom he disposes his
"grey gown," provided Martin's aesthetic tastes are not hurt.   Cf.
Ep. I. (second series) in Bonnechose's ed. of Hus' Letters.

chosen words he might have been King of Bohemia
when Wenzel died; but, as Palacky shows, his unruly
tongue cost him a throne. "We must root out Hus'
followers" had been his audacious speech to the Fathers
of Constance, and in 1419 John of Chlum and Wenzel
of Duba took care it was not forgotten.[1] The Bohemians
would have none of Sigismund for their king, and he
soon found out how hard it was to "root out" a Ziska
or a Prokop. But he was the last man to forego his
claims upon a crown without a struggle. Disdaining the
wise advice of Frederick of Brandenberg, he hastened
his fall by securing the aid of Martin V., who published
a crusade against the Hussites (1420). Had Sigismund,
late as it was, granted some concessions in matters of
religion and avoided Papal interference, he might have
created a powerful orthodox party under Cenek of
Wartenberg. But even when he pursued a worthy
object he invariably chose unworthy means. All that
the crusade did was to close the ranks of the Bohemians
against him.

The first stage of the Hussite wars comprised three
campaigns, and, in each, Ziska was an easy victor. He
had won his battles before Sigismund took the field.
Every moment wasted by the dilatory Emperor was
gain to the diligent general. The Bohemian, with the
eye of genius, grasped the situation and made preparations with the utmost care and skill. From a band
of raw peasants he created a "model" army, which, for
discipline and fearlessness, could vie with any in Europe.
John Ziska was the Oliver Cromwell of Bohemia. The
blind warrior drilled his Taborites as the Puritan trained
his Ironsides, and never once did he taste defeat. Like
the Protector he had no delicacy of tactics.[2] Like him

[1] Cf Creighton, II 45 The reference to Palacky *Documenta*
is 314

[2] Cf. Cromwell's severe Irish policy and Ziska's pillaging and

he had a grim confidence in his God-given mission, and made religious passion the basis of martial success.[1] In 1420 Sigismund with 80,000 men behind him was driven from Witkow. He fared even worse at his second venture, for, in the following year, he left 400 of his bravest nobles dead in the field of Wyssehrad; and, in 1422, his army of 90,000 men, though led by the renowned Pipo of Florence was routed at Kuttenberg.[2] The flight from Saaz was a poor attempt " to root out Hus' followers" but it was a happy inspiration for the wit of an Ebendorfer.[3]

Sigismund now had enough of crusades and Bohemia was left in peace until 1427. These five years saw the rise and fall of a Slavonic Utopia. Witold of Lithuania formed a noble scheme of a Czech Empire and Church, and sent Sigismund Korybut, nephew of Ladislas, King of Poland, into Bohemia, where he was regarded as a deliverer.[4] But Pope and Emperor were too strong for the half-hearted Poles, and when Korybut was recalled all hope of a Slav confederacy was at an end. After Ziska's death Prokop the Great became General of the Hussites, and he was the hero of the fourth and fifth crusades. In 1427 Germany became alarmed at Bohemian aggression and raised an army which laid

"Adamite" policy.   Aeneas Sylvius *Hist. Bohem.*, cc. 36-40. Cf. Windecke, 85, 206-7, 340.

[1] Cf. Ziska's words (quoted in Leger)—" we must live good lives, live as Christians, in love and fear of God, we must place in His hands our wishes, our needs, and our hopes, and wait always upon Him." Cf. also Coxe, *House of Austria*, I., 154, and his reference to Pelzel.

[2] Windecke, §§ 109, 139.

[3] Ebendorfer was one of the envoys from Basel sent to Prag. His words were: "Adeo enim eis Bohemi erant abominabiles ut non solum eos ferire sed ne quidem potuerunt eos contueri." Cf. Creighton, II., 182.

[4] For history of Korybut, cf. Windecke, §§ 103-4, 176-8, 208. Cf. Raynaldus, ann. 1427 §§ for his schemes.

siege to Mies, but the terror of Prokop and his warriors caused a shameless retreat, which even Cardinal Beaufort, crucifix in hand, could not stay. The fifth crusade ended in like disaster at Tauss (1431), for Cesarini was no more successful than Beaufort.

All hope of peace now lay in the General Council, which Martin V. had summoned to meet at Basel, with Cardinal Cesarini as its president. He, however, bequeathed the difficulties of Conciliar action to his successor, Eugenius IV., who loved the Council no more than did Martin V., and, indeed, attempted to dissolve it when Bohemian delegates were invited.[1] But Sigismund's staunch attitude, and his own quarrel with Filippo Maria Visconti reluctantly forced him to give way. A conference was held to discuss the "Four Articles," but tedious dialectic and bitter invective were its only outcome, and the delegate departed with a blessing from the generous Cesarini (April, 1433).

But Nicolas of Cusa had given a hint of compromise and there was a further conference at Prag which was more successful (Nov., 1433). The Papal delegates tried hard to incite dissension amongst the Bohemians, and joined the Calixtin nobles; but on a second visit to Prag a compromise was effected. After much labour the "Compactata" were arranged.[2] The Council gave way in the question of the Cup, and both Bohemians

[1] Cf Aeneas Sylvius *Hist. Bohem* , c. 49 Cardinal Cesarini wrote a letter to Eug IV urging him to recognise the Council It is given incompletely in Raynaldus, 1431, § 22 He says " Incitavit etiam me huc venire deformitas et dissolutio Cleri Alemaniae, ex qua laici supra modum irritantur adversus statum ecclesiasticum Propter quod valde timendum est, nisi se emendent, ne laici more Hussitarum in totum clerum irruant, ut publice dicunt . Quia revera timendum est, nisi iste clerus se corrigat, quod etiam extincta haeresi Bohemiae suscitaretur alia " For importance of letter *vide* Creighton, II , 207

[2] Creighton, II 254-60 Gieseler, V 137, quotes from Mansi's *Conc* , and gives extracts of compacts

and Moravians were allowed to receive the Eucharist in both kinds; liberty of preaching was nominally granted; discipline of the clergy was vaguely recognised, but the Council insisted upon the right of the Church and her priests to hold property.

The "Compactata" were but a temporary solution of Bohemian difficulties, and were accepted chiefly through the influence of the nobles and moderates who mourned over their country's distresses, and earnestly desired peace. But peace only came by the sword. The Taborites disdained the compromise and stood to their position on the field of battle. Bohemia, however, was to be conquered by Bohemians, as Sigismund had predicted. Prokop and his veterans were routed by an army schooled in Ziska's tactics.[1] On the field of Lipan, if not in the Dominican monastery of Basel, the Council won the day. The way was now more open for Sigismund, but the throne of Charles IV. was not an easy prize. The Emperor (for, at last, in 1433, he had acquired the honour of the title) was still suspected, and patriots who had endured the fire and blood of religious war were chary of trusting him. After negotiations at Regensburg, at Prag, and at Brunn, the "Compactata ' were signed at Iglau in July, 1436, and in August Sigismund formally entered Prag [2]

But the reconciliation was hollow, as the fate of John Rokycana clearly showed. A national policy founded upon "illusory promises" was hardly satisfactory The Emperor, however, was tired of unceasing negotiation. "I was once," he said, "a prisoner in Hungary, and save then I never was so wearied as I am now." His scruples did not prevent him from making lofty promises, and he obtained peace only a year before his death.[3]

[1] Aeneas Sylvius, *Hist Bohem* , c 51
[2] Windecke, §§ 313, 319, 322, 328, 333, 340   [3] Creighton, II 308-14

As a European question the Hussite question was at an end. All danger of a general acceptance of Hus' doctrine by Christendom had disappeared and a Catholic reaction soon set in—a reaction crowned in 1462 by the Aeneas Sylvius, who made his name at Basel. Politically, the Hussite movement was disappointing. Bohemia, indeed, withstood the influence of Germany until a strong Slavonic sentiment was born in her patriots, but the movement ended in a triumph of the nobles, despite its popular and democratic beginnings. "What did remain to Bohemia was a vigorous national vitality, a religious enthusiasm, and an austere morality."[1] Sigismund's failure in Bohemia was due to his own inordinate conceit and self-confidence, his inherent shiftiness, and his Macchiavellian diplomacy, even more than to determined religious fanaticism and hardy patriotic sentiment.

Had he been a humbler and truer man, he would have won his three crowns long before he did.

[1] Leger, *History of Austria*, pp 200-1

IV.

SIGISMUND AND EMPIRE.

SIGISMUND's career was an episode of Empire. It was his cherished scheme in 1411 to show that glory had not departed from the heritage of an Otto the Great. Men thought that Christendom was coming to an end in the beginning of the 15th century, but men were to be disappointed. Sigismund would show them how he could regain lost laurels and lead Christendom as in bygone days. He made a bold attempt, but he failed. It is hardly conceivable that a Sigismund could have been successful. The times were changed and the task would have been too much for a stronger man than the flighty Luxemburg prince. New interests had sprung up and mediaeval ideals had to give way for modern state-craft.

The remarkable expansion of Burgundy at Imperial expense was but a sign of the times.[1] The era of territorialism had begun. It was significant, too, that the cities had despaired of Empire. Though it was clearly their interest to have a strong ruler, they would support neither a Wenzel nor a Rupert, and even made common cause with the princes. Rupert, indeed, had to allow the baneful practice of armed leagues ; and the famous League of Marbach "for protection against everyone, whosoever it be" was only one of many. Had the Knights—and Sigismund had to give formal legitimation to the Imperial Knights[2]—joined with the cities, matters would have been worse, for the Swabian League showed how strong such a combination might become.

[1] Cf. above, p. 19.
[2] *Cambridge Modern History*, I., 292.

The princes, too, had strengthened their position. Aided by the Golden Bull of 1356 they had made themselves a power to be feared, and the carelessness of the Luxemburgs gave the Electoral College its great opportunity. The Electors claimed to be "the successors of the Roman Senate, if not the representatives of the Roman people as well."[1] They could depose a Wenzel and form a union at Bingen (1424) which fourteen years later dictated policy to an Albert II. and paved the way for the "Wahlkapitulation" of the 16th century.[2] The dream of a Berthold of Mainz might have been realised, had they shown no dissension. Maximilian felt their power, and Wenzel's publication of a universal "Landfriede" showed how the Empire was sore beset with war and feud,[3] to which the Speier alliance of 1381 testified, and even the Treaty of Eger, eight years later, could not check.[4]

Indeed, on all sides the Empire was threatened with dissolution, and though Sigismund could read a moral lesson to Frederick of Austria at Constance—"You know," he said with boastful pride to the Italian ambassadors, "what mighty men the Dukes of Austria are ; see now what a German King can do,"[5]—he hardly seemed to realise how nearly Frederick had succeeded. The luckless Duke had almost headed an invincible confederacy of Empire's foes in Italy, Burgundy, and Germany itself. The Swiss had decided the day for the fortunate Sigismund, but their action was ominous for the future ; and rarely were the princes united for him in later times.

So far from reviving the pretensions of Empire Sigismund's policy, a policy which the Habsburgs con-

[1] *C M H*, I , 292.   [2] *Ibid*.   [3] *Ibid*, p 294.
[4] Lodge, *Close of Middle Ages*, pp 188-90
[5] L'Enfant, I , 233-4   Cf Reichenthal, § 60, a

tinued with greater success, was to use Empire as a power outside Germany. He was called not a German king, but " King of the Romans and Hungary." His lofty schemes, therefore, for the supremacy of Empire signally failed. This was seen at the Diet of Pressburg (1430) when he was bitterly reproached for his neglect of Germany.[1] But external as his policy was, he invariably chose the wrong means. His ambition to crush the power of the Turks was a worthy aim, but surely required the help of Venice, whose interests demanded such a crusade. Yet time after time he quarrelled with the Venetians about the possession of Dalmatia. When he should have supported the Hanse against the Danes, he gave fruitless aid to Denmark. He made possible, again, an alliance between Poland and Bohemia by his sale of Newmark to the Teutonic Knights.[2]

Sigismund left the Empire weak and bequeathed a sorry legacy to Frederick III.—"astrologer, chemist, botanist, antiquary, collector, everything but ruler." Frederick's reign was "a climax of neglect of Imperial duties." Philippe de Comines could jest about the luckless Emperor,[3] and Aeneas Sylvius could make light of his authority.[4] It seemed, indeed, that the Empire was " not only dead but obsolete and a jest in Italy "; but Frederick had Sigismund to thank for much of his misfortune.

The Imperial ideal, however, was not yet dead. It inspired the exploits of an Albert Achilles and could still rouse Christendom by the memory of past glories.

---

[1] Ranke, I., 52.

[2] Lodge, p 465.

[3] He called him "the most perfectly niggardly man that ever lived." Cf. *Memoirs* (Bohn), I. 124, 245-7 ; II. 110.

[4] "Nulla ei potentia est: tantum ei paretis quantum vultis, vultis antem minimum "—quoted by Coxe, *House of Austria*, I. 213. Cf., too, Bryce, *H.R.E.*, pp. 312-5.

The same Aeneas Sylvius who could ridicule Frederick III. could still declare that the Emperor's " power is eternal . . . incapable of injury . . . no laws can bind the Emperor . . . no court judge him . . . he is answerable only to God,"[1] whilst the Emperor himself is " chased from his capital by the Hungarians, wandering from convent to convent, an Imperial beggar ; while the princes, whom his subserviency to the Pope had driven into rebellion, are offering the Imperial crown to Podiebrad, the Bohemian king."[2] As an ideal of the past, if no more, the Empire was still to hold sway.

It is remarkable, however, that notwithstanding the undoubted failure of Sigismund's Imperial policy, both Habsburgs and Hohenzollerns date their greatness from him. They were in every sense the heirs of the Luxemburg House.

As regards the more constitutional part of Sigismund's policy there is little to be said.

The crushing defeat at Brescia (1401) had shown the weakness of the German arms, and the Hussite victories had conclusively tried both military and political systems in the balance and found them wanting. The old German style of warfare had to give way for several reasons. The Middle Ages could conceive no idea save that of the heavy armed knight, but whatever such a warrior might do in the lists or in deeds of chivalry, he could not hold his own against the lightly-clad Italian mercenary. Then the army of Germany lacked unity ; in it were repeated the same traces of territorial rivalry which were destructive of the Empire itself. Gian Galeazzo's adventurers and Ziska's fanatics, too, had shown the uselessness of huge undisciplined hosts.

[1] A S, *De Ortu* Cf Bryce, *H R E*, pp 288-9 and 273 (for Alfonso's letter to Fred III). Cf. Ranke, I 54-7

[2] Bryce, *ibid*, p 289

An attempt was made to remedy this state of matters at the Diets of Frankfort.[1] In April, 1427, the wonted method of levying troops was abandoned and it was agreed that one out of every twenty should be chosen by lot. It was thought that by this means territorial jealousies would be overcome. The financial difficulty, always pressing in those times, was to be surmounted by a poll-tax on the Jews and the Papal tithes. But such good enactments did not save Germany from a disastrous flight at Mies.

Again the princes and representatives came to Frankfort (1427) and passed more advanced measures. A paid army was to be had, a general income-tax imposed (one-twentieth on the clergy, one-fourth on the laity, and a poll-tax), a war council was formed of six deputies from the Electors and three from the cities, and preparations were made for an arrangement of "circles" — an anticipation of Maximilian's constitutional reforms.[2]

Sigismund might have been more successful—for his schemes were but disappointing anticipations of later reform—had he not quarrelled with Frederick of Brandenburg, who saw that drastic reform was necessary and was yet driven into antagonism to the Emperor.[3] This alienation almost provoked a civil war after the Diet of Nürnberg (1422) and the 1424 Union of Electors, and made the reforms of Frankfort take the form of a determined opposition to Sigismund. Indeed, one outcome of the Frankfort schemes was to transfer his Imperial authority to the Council of Nine. Yet the Reform movement grew from 1433—1437, for various reasons. Bohemia was at last comparatively settled; the growing

[1] For best account of reforms *vide* Aschbach *Geschichte König Sigmunds*, I., 453, and Windecke, § 223, &c.

[2] Cf. Ranke, I , p. 111-121, &c. Cf. *C. M. H.*, I., 303-306, &c.

[3] Lodge, p. 226.

disorganisation in Germany demanded some remedy;
the Council of Basel was a stimulus to reform in the
Empire, the power of the princes was becoming felt by
clergy and cities alike; and Sigismund at last under-
stood that Imperial reform would strengthen central
power. The pamphlet of Nicolas of Cusa is interesting
as showing contemporary feeling [1]   He advocated
superior courts of justice, each provided with three
assessors chosen from the nobles, clergy, and cities;
a paid army; and, above all, yearly Diets.

But Sigismund's reforming schemes, like his other
lofty plans, came to nought. He did not give himself
whole-heartedly to reorganisation of the constitution,
but played with reform in his dealings with Pope
and Council at Basel. The Electors became tired of
their Emperor and formed a sullen neutrality which
lasted until Sigismund's death in 1437.

*   *   *   *   *   *

The Emperor loved pomp even in death. He died
on December 9 sitting on his throne, "apparelled in
magnificent attire." Himself a schemer all his days he
had the satisfaction of defeating the schemes of the
Empress on the eve of his death. He was left seated
on his throne, grave-clothes over Imperial vesture, for
three days, that men might see that the lord of all the
world was dead and gone.[2]

"These princes of the House of Luxemburg cannot
be called great kings; but they possessed buoyant and
elastic characters which never allowed them to be beaten
by any stroke of fortune. If one enterprise failed, they

[1] Ranke, I , 111-113

[2] Windecke, § 348   Also for schemes of Barbara and Count of
Cilly   Cf, for a personal description, L'Enfant, I 75-77 and reff
to Leon Aretin, Aeneas Sylvius, and Maimbourg, also Creighton,
II 316-7, who quotes Palacky

were ready with another .... They were a race not without ideas; above all, they were a race full of activity." [1] Sigismund certainly had ideas, perhaps he had too many ideas; he certainly was active and buoyant; but none of these qualities saved him from failure. They only emphasise the truth that "few men with such wise plans and such good intentions have so conspicuously failed." [2]

It is easy to laugh at Sigismund's vanity and pretensions; he was just the man to provoke laughter. But it was better that he had a soaring ambition and Quixotic schemes and yet failed, than that he should have been a mere time-server and prosaic dabbler in grovelling politics. Sigismund's failure would never have been so conspicuous, had he not aimed so high,[3] and a man does best who fails to realise his own ideals. The Emperor had a great vision of his mission in life. He could never understand that even he had to begin at the foundation of things and laboriously watch each stage in the great architecture of a world's achievements. "Ego super grammaticam" held good for him in all his undertakings and meant as much as the "L'état, c'est moi" of a Louis XIV. The bitterness of Jean de Montreuil made him a hard judge,[4] and lost much that deserved more sympathy.

Sigismund, perhaps, did not deserve success, he certainly could not command it. His lack of patience and wisdom were fatal to his cherished ideals. Yet there was something about him which attracted men. Eber-

[1] Höfler, quoted in Leger, p. 202.

[2] Creighton, II. 318.

[3] "Aiming high and generally missing" is Carlyle's epithet. Cf. I. 186.

[4] "He threatens France, Italy, all Europe, even Turkey; the very Antipodes begin to tremble"; but "parturiunt montes nascitur ridiculus mus."

hard Windecke knew him and many a time had thankless
work[1] to do for his master, yet he loved him; and
perhaps one may sympathise with his attachment.   One
may smile at Sigismund, but it is hard to hate him.

"Three crowns, Bohemia, Hungary, and the Reich,
in that one year," says the old Historian; "and then
next year he quitted them all, for a fourth and more last-
ing crown, as is hoped."[2]

[1] There must have been happier positions than that of financial
agent to Sigismund

[2] Carlyle, I , 192, n

APPENDIX.

NOTE A.

It was more by good luck than good guidance that Sigismund extorted from John XXIII. the summons of the Council of Constance. John XXIII. had been sore beset by Ladislas of Naples, and had to flee from Rome. He appealed to Sigismund, who met him at Lodi. The Pope sent his Cardinals, Zarabella and Challant, to arrange for the holding of a council, when at last he had given way to Sigismund's wishes, hoping that he could outwit the Luxemburg prince and get matters to his liking. He was too audacious, however, and found that his Cardinals (whom he released from his first instructions) had committed him to the Council at Constance where Sigismund, and not he, would be supreme.

For his ideas *vide* Leon. Aret. in *Muratori*, XIX. 928, *e.g.*, " In loco, inquit, Concilii rei summa est, nec ego alicubi esse volo, ubi Imperator plus possit. . . . . Vos, quid mihi tutum, et quid formidandum cogitetis."

Cf. L'Enfant, I. pp. 6, 8—15, 17 (*v.* Anecdote of preparations for Council and Cardinal's words, "salus huic domini," &c.).

Monstrelet, IV. 86—7.

Von der Hardt, IV. 8.

Ulrich von Reichenthal, 12, *a*.

NOTE B.

Dietrich Vrie's poem is in Von der Hardt, I. Pt. i., p. 11, and his *History of the Council of Constance*, in *Ibid.*, pp. 69, &c.

Nicholas de Clémanges probably wrote the *De Ruina Ecclesiae* (Von der Hardt, I.. Pt. iii.). There has been much controversy over the authorship. For a discussion cf. Creighton II. p. 361, n. 4. Cf. also Pastor, *History of the Popes*, I. 117, 158, and Michelet, I. 411—18, for French view of need of reform. Quotations in the text are from Von der Hardt, I., Pt. III., pp. 20—2; cf. pp. 36—8, for even graver charges.

Dietrich of Niem is the disputed author of the *De Modis Uniendi, &c.*" Von der H. ascribed it to Gerson, but cf. Pastor and Creighton *supra*.

For views of Gerson and d'Ailly *vide* Gerson, *Opera*, II. 210, seq.

NOTE C.

D'Ailly had suggested that priors, heads of congregations, doctors of Theology and Law, the King, princes, and ambassadors, should be allowed to vote (cf. Von der Hardt, II. 224. Gieseler gives extracts in IV. 290), and Cardinal Filastre had written even more vigorously, *e.g.*, "et attende, quod Rex, vel Prelatus indoctus est asinus coronatus" (Von der Hardt, II. 226). He it was who asked "quo modo deciderentur agenda in Concilio, et fieret scrutinium votorum? utrum per nationes in genere, quarum quatuor erant, ... vel per capita singula?" (Von der Hardt, II., p. 230).

For distribution into nations cf. Ceretanus in Von der Hardt, IV., II. p. 40, "Die Jovis, septima Febr., post nonnullas disceptationes decretum est, ut in Concilio per nationes, et non per vota procederetur."

NOTE D.

There are two opposing views of Sigismund's relations with France and England during the Council at Constance. Caro, *Aus der Kanzlei Kaiser Sigismunds*, cf. 128, &c., (and cf. Monstrelet, IV. 300), opposes the view of Lenz, *Konig Sigismund und Heinrich der Fünfte von England*, who declares that Sigismund's treaty with England and consequent desertion of France was determined before leaving Constance, and that he failed of reform owing to his political changes. Jean de Montreuil certainly believed this. But there is a further question: even after this, did Sigismund really gain his point in Papal Election ? It is probable that Lenz is correct here (he declares that from a Bohemian monk's semi-official account drawn up as early as 1419, he can prove that Sigismund was not beaten). The former view holds that the death of Robert Hallam changed everything, that the English deserted Sigismund after their leader was gone. But there are too many difficulties. Henry V. of England was not a man to allow his representatives to mould their own policy (cf. letter in L'Enfant, II. 98), nor was he a man to have a hap-hazard policy. Probably he wished to gain glory for himself through mediation, and by his uncle, Henry Beaufort, converted Sigismund to his view. Another difficulty, in older view, is to account for the accidental presence of Beaufort at Ulm precisely at the critical moment. Beaufort could not be always on pilgrimage to the Holy Land.

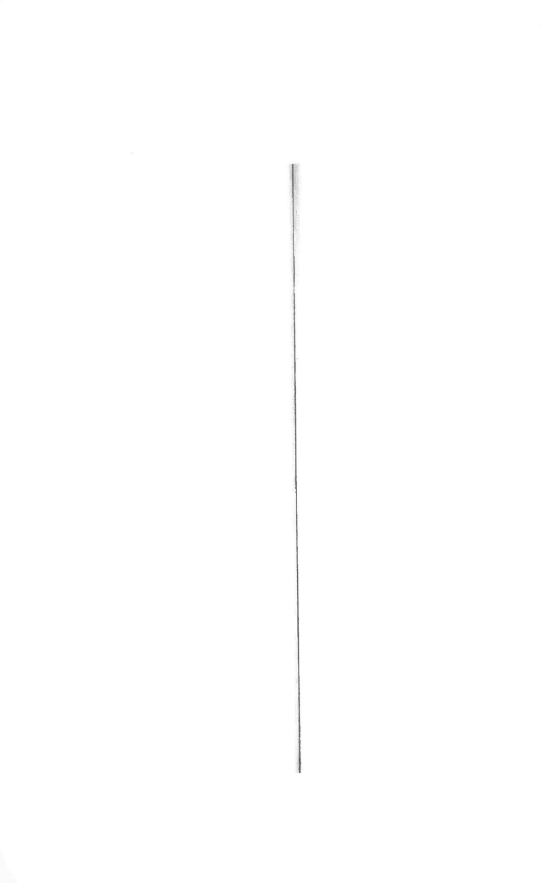

Milton Keynes UK
Ingram Content Group UK Ltd.
UKHW020841301024
2459UKWH00003B/15